GOD'S WORD
—— IS FOR ——
EVERYONE
GOD'S WORD IS FOR ME!

SARAH JANE CONAWAY, AUTHOR

KAREN MILLIGAN, EDITOR

TABLE OF CONTENTS

GOD'S WORD IS FOR EVERYONE

The Bible—God's Word—is for everyone.
Make the title personal.

GOD'S WORD IS FOR ME!

Now, repeat the above statement seven times. Let it sink into your soul. You have currently said, "God's Word is for ME!" seven times. So whenever you feel confused about a passage, remember this statement. Sometimes it takes days, weeks, months even years to come to an understanding of a certain passage from the Bible. Don't expect to understand everything you read the first time you read it. Understanding comes with growth in your Christian life.

God's Word has become my reason for living. As a young teenager, I wanted His will for my life. I found His will by reading His Word. When I began reading the Bible, I was a very poor reader and I read very slowly. I did not understand the meaning of many words. As I matured into adulthood the Lord guided me to have a closer walk with Him by causing something to happen that I was not ready for – teaching my own sons. Teaching my oldest son phonics caused me to learn phonics. It gave me an ability that I had been lacking – reading well with understanding! Reading brought me closer to the Lord, because I could understand His message to me. I am still learning from my loving Saviour as I read His Word.

You can too. Maybe I am writing this for others like myself, who had been taught sight reading in place of phonics. If this is you, then find a YouTube video teaching phonics or help out in a Christian school in their learning-to-read class and learn phonics discretely.

There are Christians who have never thought about reading God's Message for themselves. Have you ever asked yourself what you need to do to make your life more complete? God knows us better than we know ourselves. He knows what talents are hidden deep inside of us that need to come out. Sometimes God uses His Word to allow our talents to surface. For instance, my author career began in 2015. My first book was published in March 2016. I was at the young age of 66. Never did I dream of becoming an author. That was something that only God knew! Through my study of the Bible, God revealed to me what He wanted for my life.

Anyone who reads the Bible needs to know the Author. I am talking about trusting Jesus Christ as your Saviour. Jesus suffered very cruel punishment and death and rose from the grave so that you and I can live forever with Him. 1st Thessalonians 5:10 reads,

Who died for us, that, whether we wake or sleep, we should live together with him.

You simply need to acknowledge that you are in the category of sinner. Romans 3:23 states,

For all have sinned, and come short of the glory of God;

Jesus took your place in death so that you could live forever with Him in Heaven. Just accept what He did for you by faith. Ephesians 2:8–9 states,

> *For by grace are ye saved through faith; and that not of yourselves: it is the gift of God: Not of works, lest any man should boast.*

When we accept Jesus by faith, the Holy Spirit comes to live in us and becomes our teacher.

The Bible – God's Word – is a spiritual book so it is understandable to have the Holy Spirit (Holy Ghost) as our guide. John 14:26,

> *But the Comforter, which is the Holy Ghost, whom the Father will send in my name, he shall teach you all things, and bring all things to your remembrance, whatsoever I have said unto you.*

BIBLE READING PLANS

When we begin reading The Word of God, we need to understand that we should always have a plan. We need to realize that:

This Book covers all of life.
This Book is different from all other books.
This Book is a library of books.

You can start anywhere in this library. The Bible is divided into two sections, the Old Testament and the New Testament. It is best to start in the New Testament. For the new reader and the new Christian, the New Testament is easier to understand. I have several plans that are not original with me. About forty years ago I read the book <u>How to Study the Bible for Yourself</u> by Tim LaHaye. I adapted his plans to fit my reading ability at the time.

He suggests that you start in 1st John. It is a short book written by John the beloved, an apostle of Jesus Christ. It is located in the back of the New Testament – fifth book from the back. (If you have trouble finding these books, go to the Table of Contents in the front of the Bible. It will give you the page number.) The plan is to read the book, 1st John, seven times. Then you go to John, the fourth book in the New Testament, and read it twice. Next, read Mark twice as well. At the end of this article, there are programs available for copying.

Brother LaHaye suggests a time frame for each section, but at that time I could not read fast enough to fit into it. I suggest that you put your start date at the top of the page, then your finish date at the bottom of the page. I have done this program several times and I can now do it within Brother LaHaye's time frame.

I suggest that those of you who are just beginning the habit of reading your Bible on a daily basis to concentrate on becoming habitual in reading. Whether you read one chapter or several chapters daily, in my opinion, is not important. The important thing is that you read something from the plan. Satan will fight you. That is an undeniable fact. He will put things in your way to keep you from reading God's Word. Ask the Lord to remind you to read, then if you happen to forget, He will remind you. He did it for me. Follow the plan until you finish it. Keep a record by marking the chapter numbers as you read. If you miss one day or a whole week, you know just exactly where you left off. Take it from there.

Permit me to share a little history from my own journey in establishing my habit of reading daily from the Word of God. As a teen I tried to read my Bible daily, but I was unsuccessful. I did work at memorizing Scripture. I worked hard at it. At our church we were involved with a program that rewarded children and adults for memorizing five verses per week. One particular day I was ready to say my verses at church but decided to repeat them to my father first. With confidence and a rather loud voice I began "Psalm 139:23–24 Stretch me, O God…" At that point my parents doubled over into fits of laughter. Mom said, "Janie, sometimes I think I need the Lord to stretch me." After the laughter settled down, they told me that the word was Search. I was so thankful that I practiced one more time at home before saying it at church. By the way, the verses correctly stated are:

Search me, O God, and know my heart: try me, and know my thoughts: And see if there be any wicked way in me, and lead me in the way everlasting.

These verses have become my prayer-time request to my Lord and Saviour.

My desire to serve the Lord led me to my husband, Ron. He was a good reader. We were the same age but somewhere along in his childhood he learned phonics. From him I began to really see the need to read my Bible daily. He read multiple chapters in the same length of time I could read one. I started reading one chapter daily beginning in Genesis. Now this is not a read-through-the-Bible-in one-year program. There are 1,189 chapters in the Bible. Divide that number by 365 and you get approximately 3.25 years. That means, IF a person reads one chapter daily, then it would take three years and three months, more or less to get the job done. However, I was just beginning and I did not read daily. I kept a marker in my Bible so I would know where I was to read the next time. There were days missed and sometimes weeks. I figure that even though I did not keep a record of my start date and my finish date, it probably took somewhere around 4 to 5 years to complete my first read-through of the Bible.

Another way that helped me to become faithful in reading daily was to keep a record of my daily Scripture reading on a calendar. The calendar was printed on a sheet of printer paper. When I read the chapters, I would x out the chapter number and if I missed the day of reading I made a big X on the date box. At the end of the month I would count how many days the Lord got my attention and the number of days Satan interfered. At that moment, I would thank the Lord for the days that I succeeded in reading His Word and ask Him to remind me to read every day. On those months that I read more days for the Lord, I would laugh out loud at Satan and tell him that he lost. Gradually the days missed became fewer and fewer. Praise the Lord! Remember this—the Lord wants you to KNOW HIM! He wants to be first in your life. Make getting to know Him personal, make it fun.

There are many suggestions as to where to start reading the Bible. Most of the programs begin with Genesis and Matthew at the same time to finish in one year. This I knew was not for me at that time. As mentioned above, the book How to Study the Bible for Yourself taught me so much about reading the Bible as well as studying it. I have put into practice a lot of it but there is always something more I can learn when I re-read it or teach it.

The Bible is such a unique book that you can start almost anywhere in it. The seasoned reader can decide to read about history in the Old Testament and choose from the five books of Moses or in the New Testament the book of Acts. Ruth and Esther are good books to read for enjoyment and study. The important thing is to read in a systematic way. Take the book of Acts for instance. Start in chapter one and read your designated number of chapters daily until you finish chapter 28. Once you are accustomed to reading daily, use your imagination to form your own plan.

Several years ago I decided to read Psalms and Proverbs daily finishing both in one month every month. However, I read Psalm 119 separately. I read two of the eight verse sections daily finishing it in eleven days. Then I started over again. It is usually completed 2–3 times a month. Proverbs is read according to the corresponding day of the month. Proverbs ˊ on the first day of the month, etc. In months that have less than 31 days just read chapters 30 and 31 on the thirtieth of the month. February needs three days of doubling up. Psalms divides nicely into 5 Psalms daily – chapters 1–5 on the first then 6–10 on the 2nd and so forth. Those months that have 31 days you can omit reading Psalms or the 31st and start again on the first of the next month.

After you have gone through the plans as I have given them to you, be creative, be open to what the Lord wants you to read. Just read the Bible daily. I promise, you will be blessed by it.

BIBLE READING PROGRAM 1

Beginning date _____

Read each book in the order listed. The numbers after each book are the chapter numbers. Cross out the number of the chapter after you have read it.

I John	1 2 3 4 5	1 2 3 4 5
	1 2 3 4 5	1 2 3 4 5
	1 2 3 4 5	1 2 3 4 5
	1 2 3 4 5	

John   1 2 3 4 5 6 7 8 9 10 11 12 13 14 15 16
        17 18 19 20 21

        1 2 3 4 5 6 7 8 9 10 11 12 13 14 15 16
        17 18 19 20 21

Mark   1 2 3 4 5 6 7 8 9 10 11 12 13 14 15 16

        1 2 3 4 5 6 7 8 9 10 11 12 13 14 15 16

Galatians   1 2 3 4 5 6

Ephesians   1 2 3 4 5 6

Philippians   1 2 3 4

Colossians   1 2 3 4

1 Thessalonians	1 2 3 4 5
2 Thessalonians	1 2 3
1 Timothy	1 2 3 4 5 6
2 Timothy	1 2 3 4
Titus	1 2 3
Philemon	1
Luke	1 2 3 4 5 6 7 8 9 10 11 12 13 14 15 16 17 18 19 20 21 22 23 24
Acts	1 2 3 4 5 6 7 8 9 10 11 12 13 14 15 16 17 18 19 20 21 22 23 24 25 26 27 28
Romans	1 2 3 4 5 6 7 8 9 10 11 12 13 14 15 16

Ending date _____

BIBLE READING PROGRAM 2

Beginning date _____

Read the entire New Testament twice.

Matthew	1 2 3 4 5 6 7 8 9 10 11 12 13 14 15 16 17 18 19 20 21 22 23 24 25 26 27 28
Mark	1 2 3 4 5 6 7 8 9 10 11 12 13 14 15 16
Luke	1 2 3 4 5 6 7 8 9 10 11 12 13 14 15 16 17 18 19 20 21 22 23 24
John	1 2 3 4 5 6 7 8 9 10 11 12 13 14 15 16 17 18 19 20 21
Acts	1 2 3 4 5 6 7 8 9 10 11 12 13 14 15 16 17 18 19 20 21 22 23 24 25 26 27 28
Romans	1 2 3 4 5 6 7 8 9 10 11 12 13 14 15 16
1 Corinthians	1 2 3 4 5 6 7 8 9 10 11 12 13 14 15 16
2 Corinthians	1 2 3 4 5 6 7 8 9 10 11 12 13
Galatians	1 2 3 4 5 6
Ephesians	1 2 3 4 5 6
Philippians	1 2 3 4
Colossians	1 2 3 4

1 Thessalonians	1 2 3 4 5
2 Thessalonians	1 2 3 4
1 Timothy	1 2 3 4 5 6
2 Timothy	1 2 3 4
Titus	1 2 3
Philemon	1
Hebrews	1 2 3 4 5 6 7 8 9 10 11 12 13
James	1 2 3 4 5
1 Peter	1 2 3 4 5
2 Peter	1 2 3
1 John	1 2 3 4 5
2 John	1
3 John	1
Jude	1
Revelations	1 2 3 4 5 6 7 8 9 10 11 12 13 14 15 16 17 18 19 20 21 22

Ending date _____

Now read the New Testament again, before going to program 3.

BIBLE READING PROGRAM 3— WISDOM LITERATURE READING

Beginning date _____

Read 1 chapter in Proverbs daily that coincides with the calendar date. You will also read 2 chapters in the four other wisdom books of the Old Testament daily. This one is more structured – reading Proverbs repeatedly for four months.

Proverbs
1 2 3 4 5 6 7 8 9 10 11 12 13 14 15
16 17 18 19 20 21 22 23 24 25 26 27
28 29 30 31

1 2 3 4 5 6 7 8 9 10 11 12 13 14 15
16 17 18 19 20 21 22 23 24 25 26 27
28 29 30 31

1 2 3 4 5 6 7 8 9 10 11 12 13 14 15
16 17 18 19 20 21 22 23 24 25 26 27
28 29 30 31

1 2 3 4 5 6 7 8 9 10 11 12 13 14 15
16 17 18 19 20 21 22 23 24 25 26 27
28 29 30 31

Job
1 2 3 4 5 6 7 8 9 10 11 12 13 14 15
16 17 18 19 20 21 22 23 24 25 26 27

28 29 30 31 32 33 34 35 36 37 38 39
40 41 42

Psalms

1 2 3 4 5 6 7 8 9 10 11 12 13 14 15
16 17 18 19 20 21 22 23 24 25 26 27
28 29 30 31 32 33 34 35 36 37 38 39
40 41 42 43 44 45 46 47 48 49 50 51
52 53 54 55 56 57 58 59 60 61 62 63
64 65 66 67 68 69 70 71 72 73 74 75
76 77 78 79 80 81 82 83 84 85 86 87
88 89 90 91 92 93 94 95 96 97 98 99
100 101 102 103 104 105 106 107 108
109 110 111 112 113 114 115 116 117
118 119 120 121 122 123 124 125 126
127 128 129 130 131 132 133 134 135
136 137 138 139 140 141 142 143 144
145 146 147 148 149 150

Ecclesiastes

1 2 3 4 5 6 7 8 9 10 11 12

Song of
Solomon

1 2 3 4 5 6 7 8

Ending date _____

BIBLE READING PROGRAM 4

Beginning date _____

Read repeatedly each book or passage for one month. Brother LaHaye recommends these to give you a good foundation in the content found in them. However, you can adjust this to whatever passages or short books meet your spiritual needs. These suggested books will take 8 months. For instance read 1st John every day for one month then read Ephesians for one month etc.

1 John

Ephesians

Philippians

Colossians

1 Thessalonians

James

Romans   5–8

John   14–7

Ending date _____

BIBLE READING PROGRAM 5

Beginning date _____

Read through the Bible: Genes s – Revelations

The suggestion is:

One New Testament chapter daily Monday – Saturday
Two Old Testament chapters daily Monday – Saturday
Five Old Testament chapters on Sunday

Ending date _____

This is adaptable to your schedule and your reading ability. Make reading the Bible fun not a chore. However, if it feels like a chore, tell the Lord about it. He will help you with His ideas. Listen to Him. Do not compare yourself to others. This is between you and your Lord.

I have thoroughly enjoyed sharing my history with you in learning to read God's Word. Read the Bible and enjoy yourself while doing it. I am praying for you.

"Lord, put your loving arms around those who read this little book. Help them to realize your love for them. Guide them in reading your precious Book. In Jesus Name, Amen."

Your friend,
Jane
sarahjane@auntjane.ws

Please, let me know how this book has helped you. Then I can pray for you by name. Thank you.

OTHER BOOKS BY SARAH JANE CONAWAY

Declare His Glory:
Preparations for Life on the Mission Field

The author tells how she and her husband rose victoriously over the adversities and went on to serve on the mission field for many decades.

Becky P.

On this missionary calling, great preparations ahead of time were hectic for Sarah Jane and her husband, Pastor Ron. Both of them passed God's challenges in the right time and in proper direction. Forty years in a ministry, Sarah Jane Conaway stood up to continue to set affections on her mission of God's calling in Mexico…

Verified Amazon Review

This book opened my eyes to some great truths! Loved to read this book and couldn't put it down!

Elizabeth

This little book will inspire, motivate, and encourage any Christian young or old. It takes determined conviction to pursue the call on each of our lives.

Joan B.

Joseph and Jonah:
A Faithful Servant and Runaway Preacher

I love how the Bible shows the full spectrum of human behavior. These 2 characters the author chose beautifully demonstrate the extremes. I believe any reader will be blessed and challenged by this book.

Debbie B.

This is an easy to read and interesting book comparing two men of the Bible. The end of each chapter gives a thought or question that helps us analyze our own lives and apply the truths she presents to ourselves.

Gerri J.

THE BIRTH OF CHRIST COLORING BOOK SERIES
For children 4–10 years of age

Book 1 – *Zacharias: The Man Who Lost His Voice*

The two storybooks I purchased went to my grandsons, 3 & 8. The Bible story was clear and easy to understand and the illustrations were perfect for coloring!

Kurt W.

My boys really like this book and it was a great read for all of us at bedtime, along with our other Bible stories we read.

Jenni O.

Book 2 – Mary: And Her Heavenly Visitor

As a proud grandpa, I'm thoroughly pleased to know my grandsons are getting Bible truth in a stimulating and fun format that's perfect for their age levels.

Kurt W.

Book 3 – John: Son of the Man Who Lost His Voice

Book 4: Jesus: The Shepherds Visit Baby Jesus

Book 5: The Wise Men:
Visitors from the East Meet Jesus, the Toddler

You can purchase these books at
https://www.amazon.com/author/sarahjane

www.ingramcontent.com/pod-product-compliance
Lightning Source LLC
Chambersburg PA
CBHW070756050426
42449CB00010B/2499